Just the Facts
Refugees
Steven Maddocks

Heinemann
LIBRARY

www.heinemann.co.uk/library

Visit our website to find out more information about **Heinemann Library** books.

To order:

 Phone 44 (0) 1865 888066

 Send a fax to 44 (0) 1865 314091

 Visit the Heinemann Bookshop at www.heinemann.co.uk/library to browse our catalogue and order online.

Produced by Monkey Puzzle Media Ltd
Gissing's Farm, Fressingfield, Suffolk IP21 5SH, UK

First published in Great Britain by Heinemann Library, Halley Court, Jordan Hill, Oxford OX2 8EJ, part of Harcourt Education.
Heinemann is a registered trademark of Harcourt Education Ltd.

Editorial: Sarah Eason and Georga Godwin
Design: Mayer Media
Picture Research: Lynda Lines
Consultant: Ian Derbyshire
Production: Edward Moore

Originated by Dot Gradations Ltd
Printed and bound in Hong Kong, China by
  South China Printing Company

ISBN 0 431 16163 1
08 07 06 05 04
10 9 8 7 6 5 4 3 2 1

British Library Cataloguing in Publication Data
Maddocks, Steven
Refugees
325.2'1
A full catalogue record for this book is available from the British Library.

Acknowledgements
The publishers would like to thank the following for permission to reproduce photographs:
AKG London p. **13**; Alamy p. **10** (Popperfoto); Art Archive p. **9 top** (Duomo di Sangimignano/ Dagli Orti); Associated Press p. **19** (Antonio d'Urso); Corbis pp. **5** (Joseph Sohn/Chromosohm Inc), **9 bottom** (Bettmann); Exile Images pp. **14** (H. Davies), **17** (H. Davies), **27** (H. Davies), **31** (H. Davies), **45** (R. Chalasani); Panos Pictures pp. **35** (Chris Stowers), **38 bottom** (Howard Davies), **40** (Giacomo Pirozzi), **42** (Andy Johnstone), **43** J.C. Tordai), **47** (Liba Taylor); Popperfoto/Reuters pp. **16, 32–33, 46**; Press Association p. **4** (EPA); Rex Features pp. **11** (Sipa), **23** (Wilhemsen), **26** (James Fraser); Still Pictures pp. **6–7** (Heine Pedersen), **22** (Hartmut Schwarzbach), **24** (Peter Frischmuth), **25** (Mathias Heng), **28–29** (J. Dago/UNEP), **38 top** (Jorgen Schytte), **41** (Heine Pedersen); UNHCR pp. **20, 21, 37, 48**.

Cover photograph reproduced with permission of UNHCR.

Every effort has been made to contact copyright holders of any material reproduced in this book. Any omissions will be rectified in subsequent printings if notice is given to the publishers.

Any words appearing in the text in bold, **like this**, are explained in the Glossary.

362.87 MAD

X

Contents

Introduction

Refugees are people who have been forced to run away from their homes because their lives are in danger, and who cannot return because they fear they will be tortured, imprisoned or killed. One of the main reasons that people become refugees is that they are being **persecuted** – treated with violence and prejudice because of their race or religion or their political beliefs. People who are persecuted are, in many cases, forced out of their homes and are denied access to social services, such as education and healthcare. They live with the continual threat of violence and even death.

In dozens of countries, governments do not protect all of their citizens from persecution, and in some countries, the government actively persecutes some of its citizens. What option is there for people who are seen as enemies by their own government, except to escape?

Different definitions

In 1950, the United Nations (**UN**) formed an agency specially to deal with refugees. It was known as the Office of the High Commissioner for Refugees, or **UNHCR** for short. The following year, UNHCR held an international meeting and agreed on a definition for 'refugees'. The result was a document called the 1951 **Convention** Relating to the Status of Refugees. All the countries that signed the Convention agreed to take in refugees and to ensure their safety. They also agreed on an official definition of a refugee as someone who 'owing to a well-founded fear of being persecuted for reasons of race, religion, nationality, membership of a particular social group, or political opinion, is outside the country of his

Refugees from war-torn Afghanistan make the desperate journey to claim food and shelter in a temporary relief camp in Pakistan.

nationality'. But many people believe that this definition is too limited. Persecution is a major reason for people becoming refugees, but many are also forced to leave their homes because they are fleeing from conflicts, such as wars or revolutions, or from natural disasters, like floods, earthquakes or **droughts**. According to the 1951 official definition, a person who has run away from war is not a refugee. Neither is a person whose home has been buried by a mudslide, or people who have fled for their lives but stayed in their own country.

Today, representatives of UNHCR argue that there should be a broader definition of refugees than the one given in 1951. However, many of the most powerful countries in the UN claim that their countries are unable to take in any more refugees, and so they do not want a broader definition. The governments of these countries are also concerned that some of the people who arrive in their countries are not genuine refugees.

An enormous problem

In January 2002, there were around twenty million refugees. Eighty per cent of these were women, children or the elderly, and almost half were children under eighteen. Refugees have left behind their homes, their possessions, their jobs and often their loved ones. Escape may have saved them for the time being, but they face hardship in a new culture, which can often be hostile and unwelcoming to them. Refugees are people in desperate circumstances.

**"Give me your tired, your poor,
Your huddled masses yearning to breathe free,
The wretched refuse of your teeming shore.
Send these, the homeless, tempest-tost to me."**

Poem by US poet Emma Lazarus (1849-87), on a plaque beneath the Statue of Liberty (left), welcoming refugees to the USA. For hundreds of years, people flocked to America, but now the USA does not take in such large numbers of refugees.

Where to run?

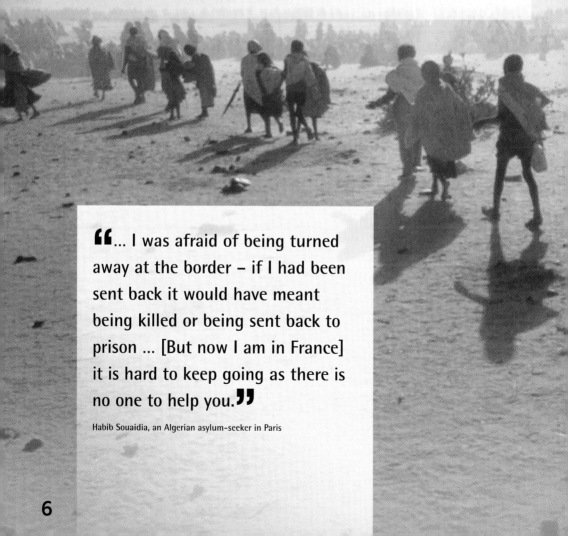

Refugees usually come from very poor countries. When they are forced to escape from their own country, most of them do not have enough money to travel far, so their only option is to make a desperate dash for the nearest national border. But many of the bordering countries are themselves ravaged by **civil war**, disease or terrible poverty. Of the ten countries with the greatest numbers of refugees, eight are struggling to look after their own populations. To be a refugee in one of these struggling countries is not a good prospect. Often, refugees will try to travel further, and reach a **host country** that can offer a better life to them and their children. Understandably, many refugees try to reach a rich country, such as the UK, the USA or Australia.

❝... I was afraid of being turned away at the border – if I had been sent back it would have meant being killed or being sent back to prison ... [But now I am in France] it is hard to keep going as there is no one to help you.**❞**

Habib Souaidia, an Algerian asylum-seeker in Paris

Asylum-seekers

As well as providing a definition of refugees, the 1951 **UN Convention** Relating to the Status of Refugees also sets out the rights of refugees. It has been signed by 144 countries, and refugees are permitted to apply for **asylum** in any of these countries. Asylum means 'safety' and an **asylum-seeker** is someone who is seeking a place of safety. If an asylum-seeker is successful, they will be allowed to live in their host country, and in some cases, after a certain time, will be able to apply for full **citizenship** of that country. In principle, all refugees who present themselves to the authorities within one of the 144 countries have certain rights. They must not be put in prison, and must not be sent back to their country of origin until the danger has passed. In practice, many asylum-seekers fail to gain the protection of the government of a host country. Even those who succeed in gaining asylum often face **discrimination**, **persecution** and violent attacks – the very things they were running away from.

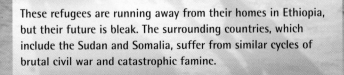

These refugees are running away from their homes in Ethiopia, but their future is bleak. The surrounding countries, which include the Sudan and Somalia, suffer from similar cycles of brutal civil war and catastrophic famine.

Early refugees

There have been refugees in the world for as long as groups of people have been trying to conquer other people's land. In ancient times, the lands surrounding the Mediterranean were home to many powerful empires. These great powers often invaded each other's territory, causing many people to flee from their homelands.

Driven from their homeland

The best known example of refugees in early history is that of the Jews. In 586 BCE, the Babylonian people invaded the kingdom of Judah and expelled the Jews. For many years, the Jewish community lived in Babylonia – the area that is now southern Iraq. They kept their traditions alive and dreamed of returning to their homeland. When the Babylonians were in turn conquered by the Persians, the Jews finally returned home.

Another group of people driven from their homeland were the ancient Britons. In the 5th century CE, Britain was invaded by Saxon armies. Large numbers of Britons left their homes and escaped to remote parts of the country. Before they left, they buried hoards of coins and valuables, clearly hoping to come back one day and dig up their wealth.

The attachment to a homeland is deeply rooted in human nature. For many communities, the sense of their homeland is an inseparable part of the identity of the people who live there.

Religious persecution

From the 16th century onwards, there were many example of religious **persecution** in Europe, as different groups of Christians disagreed about the best way to worship. In some countries, the Protestants, who had broken away from the Catholic Church in the 1520s and did not recognize the Pope as their leader, were persecuted by the Catholics.

In the early 1700s, Protestants living in western Germany were persecuted by a group of Catholics, who forced them to leave their homeland. Many of these German Protestants headed for England, which was also a Protestant country. The German refugees were invited to England by Queen Anne. She expected a few hundred, but 13,000 arrived within a few days. They were exhausted, starving and penniless.

The German refugees kept their sense of community and identity alive by practising their own religion in their own language. Meanwhile a debate

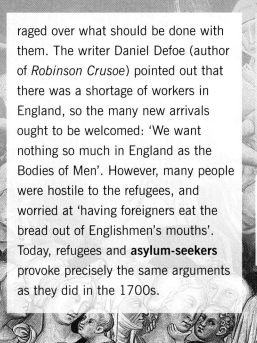

raged over what should be done with them. The writer Daniel Defoe (author of *Robinson Crusoe*) pointed out that there was a shortage of workers in England, so the many new arrivals ought to be welcomed: 'We want nothing so much in England as the Bodies of Men'. However, many people were hostile to the refugees, and worried at 'having foreigners eat the bread out of Englishmen's mouths'. Today, refugees and **asylum-seekers** provoke precisely the same arguments as they did in the 1700s.

"By the rivers of Babylon, there we sat down, and there we wept, when we remembered Zion."

Psalm 137, *The Bible* (Revised Standard Version)
During their time as refugees in Babylon in the 6th century BCE, the Jews dreamed of returning to their homeland, which they called Zion. This famous passage from the Bible describes their feelings.

In the 13th century BCE, the Jews escaped from Egypt, where they were persecuted and kept as slaves. This picture shows the Jewish people watching as the waters of the Red Sea part miraculously to help them escape.

Many of the early settlers in America were refugees fleeing from religious persecution in Europe. Here Dutch settlers are shown landing on Manhattan Island in the 17th century.

9

Recent refugees

Sometimes people are **persecuted** because of their race. The worst ever example of racial persecution took place in the first half of the 20th century. During the 1930s, Adolf Hitler and his **Nazi** party began the appalling persecution of German Jews. Hitler blamed the Jews for many of the social problems in Germany, and claimed he wanted Germany to be 'racially pure'. In 1935, Hitler's Nuremberg Laws deprived Jews of the right to vote and to hold public office and made it illegal for a Jew to marry a non-Jew.

As a result of this persecution, hundreds of thousands of Jews – along with Hitler's political opponents and other **ethnic minorities**, such as gypsies – were forced to run away. Those who stayed were imprisoned, tortured and killed. Among the Jews who fled from Nazi Germany were the **psychoanalyst** Sigmund Freud and the scientist Albert Einstein, two of the most important figures of the 20th century.

In December 1938, shortly before the outbreak of World War II, a steamship brought 502 young refugees from Vienna, Austria, to the UK. Four hundred of them were Jewish and the remainder belonged to other religious and ethnic minorities who were threatened by the Nazis.

From rags to riches

Many refugees who settle permanently in a new country make a significant contribution to the country that welcomes them. In 1849, Karl Marx, the German social historian and economist, was accused of stirring up an armed revolution against the **Prussian** king. Although he was not guilty, he was **exiled** from Prussian territories and spent the last 34 years of his life in London. It was during this period that he published his famous work, *Das Kapital*. This book was the foundation of **communism**.

In Leeds (northern England) in 1884, a Jewish refugee from Poland called Michael Marks set up a market stall called Marks' Penny Bazaar. From humble beginnings, this grew into Marks & Spencer, one of the UK's best known and most successful department stores.

In 1939, after the Nazis occupied Czechoslovakia, the Korbel family fled to England with their two-year-old daughter Madeleine. They returned to Czechoslovakia in 1945, but three years later, they were made refugees again when Czechoslovakia was taken over by the communist party. In the 1960s, Madeleine Korbel married Joseph Albright, and began a career in international affairs. In 1993, US President Bill Clinton made Madeleine Albright US **ambassador** to the **UN**, and in 1997 she became the first female **Secretary of State** in US history.

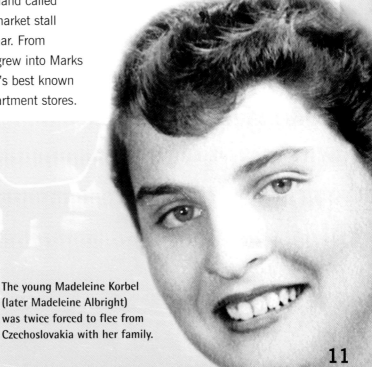

The young Madeleine Korbel (later Madeleine Albright) was twice forced to flee from Czechoslovakia with her family.

Refugees and war

Until the 19th century, refugee numbers were relatively small, but around 1850, wars in Europe increased in scale and intensity. Fighting devastated towns, villages and large areas of countryside. National borders were drawn and redrawn, and ever greater numbers of people were **displaced** from their homes.

World War I (1914–18)

World War I was fought on a scale never before witnessed. Numbers of refugees in Europe shot up to around four million as people were driven from their homes as a result of the fighting between the Allied powers (including Russia, France and the UK) and the Central powers (Germany, Austro-Hungary and Turkey). World War I also led to widespread famine and poverty throughout Europe, and even more people were faced with the terrible choice between running away or dying.

The League of Nations

In 1920, two years after World War I ended, an international organization known as the League of Nations was set up to make sure that such a war would never happen again. Refugees had become such a serious problem that in 1921 the League appointed a High Commissioner for Refugees. He was Fridtjof Nansen, a Norwegian explorer and scientist.

Nansen realized that the majority of refugees were stranded in a foreign country with no legal papers, and therefore no possibility of crossing a border and returning home. He devised the 'Nansen Passport', which provided a secure **legal status** for refugees, and ensured that it was recognized throughout the world. The Nansen Passport gave the world's unwanted people an identity and allowed hundreds of thousands to begin their long journey home.

Nansen's work to aid refugees escaping from famine in southern Russia earned him the Nobel Peace Prize in 1922.

World War II (1939–45)

Despite the efforts of the League of Nations, a world war did happen again, and on an even more terrifying scale. By the end of World War II, over forty million people in Europe had been displaced. But the war did not just affect Europe. There were refugee problems around the globe, in South-east Asia, China and Palestine.

UNHCR

In 1950, the United Nations, the successor to the League of Nations, established the Office of the United Nations High Commission for Refugees (**UNHCR**). Today, UNHCR is one of the world's principal aid agencies. Its staff of more than 5000 helps around twenty million people in more than 120 countries. During its first half-century of work, the agency provided assistance to at least fifty million people, earning two Nobel Peace Prizes in 1954 and 1981.

In 1943, Soviet refugees braved the freezing Russian winter and left their homes to seek safety, shelter and survival elsewhere.

A growing problem

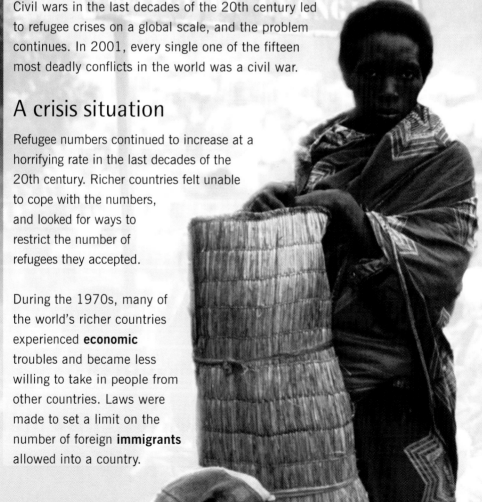

Civil wars

By the end of the 20th century, most of the conflicts in the world were **civil wars**. Civil wars are fought between different groups inside a country, often in towns and cities instead of on a traditional battlefield. This means that many innocent people are caught up in the fighting and are in danger of losing their homes. Civil wars are usually fought in very poor countries, and as well as killing thousands, the fighting also devastates the countryside. One of the most appalling civil wars took place in 1994 in the central African country of Rwanda (see case study opposite).

Civil wars in the last decades of the 20th century led to refugee crises on a global scale, and the problem continues. In 2001, every single one of the fifteen most deadly conflicts in the world was a civil war.

A crisis situation

Refugee numbers continued to increase at a horrifying rate in the last decades of the 20th century. Richer countries felt unable to cope with the numbers, and looked for ways to restrict the number of refugees they accepted.

During the 1970s, many of the world's richer countries experienced **economic** troubles and became less willing to take in people from other countries. Laws were made to set a limit on the number of foreign **immigrants** allowed into a country.

Many people think that these immigration laws should have only applied to 'voluntary' immigrants – people who had freely chosen to leave their homelands. However, in many cases they were applied to refugees as well.

As well as limiting the number of immigrants that they took into their country, many of the world's richer countries also made the process of claiming **asylum** more difficult. Generally, **asylum-seekers** would file their claim from a distance – often in the **embassy** or **consulate** of the country that they wanted to move to. If the claim was accepted, the asylum-seeker could be given permission to make the journey. However, asylum-seekers began to feel that these claims were being ignored. Many decided that the only way that they could get their asylum case heard in another country was to go there – by any means possible.

From the 1970s onwards, huge waves of refugees, sometimes thousands at a time, arrived in the USA, Europe and Australia, hoping to gain asylum. In many cases they were turned away. Unwanted or in danger in their homelands, these refugees became the unwanted of the world.

Case study
Civil war in Rwanda

In 1994, tension between the two main **ethnic groups** in Rwanda (central Africa) – the Hutu and the Tutsi – erupted into horrific violence. Hundreds of thousands of Tutsis escaped over the border into Burundi and Tanzania. But an even greater refugee crisis developed when the Tutsis regained control of Rwanda and around two million Hutus fled into **exile**. A million crossed into Goma, in Zaire (now the Democratic Republic of the Congo) in five days. At 10,000 people an hour, this was the fastest **exodus** of people from a country ever recorded.

The Rwandan civil war was one of the bloodiest and most vicious conflicts ever known. This Rwandan refugee waits to cross the border into Zaire (the Democratic Republic of the Congo).

Desperate journeys

Many refugees are so desperate to escape from their homeland, that they undertake incredibly difficult and dangerous journeys to reach another country – even though there is no guarantee that they will be allowed to stay in the new country.

There are countless stories of desperate journeys undertaken by refugees. The following journeys all took place in 2001. In July, two refugees from Lithuania (a small country in Eastern Europe) were caught trying to cross from France to England in an inflatable dinghy. They were paddling with their hands. In ten hours they travelled only 11 kilometres (9 miles). In March, nine gypsies from Romania (in Eastern Europe), including two pregnant women and a three-year-old girl, hid under a high-speed train. They stayed hidden for three hours as the train raced from Paris to London at speeds of up to 300 kph, including a stretch through the Channel Tunnel.

In June 2001, Mohammed Ayaz tried to escape from a harsh life on the border of Pakistan and Afghanistan by hiding in the wheelbay of an aeroplane bound for London. He clearly did not know that, when the plane was 10,000 metres above the Earth, and travelling at 800 kph, the temperature would fall to minus 40 °C. As the plane came into land, the pilot lowered the wheels. Ayaz, who was probably already dead, fell 7000 metres on to a supermarket car park. On the other hand, in 1996, Indian refugee Pardeep Saini miraculously survived a ten-hour flight from Delhi to London hidden in the wheelbay of an aeroplane.

Every year, some African refugees, like these men from Nigeria and the Ivory Coast, try to cross the Mediterranean in tiny boats. Many of them do not survive the journey.

Case study
Azad's journey

The largest group of refugees seeking **asylum** in the UK in recent years has been the Kurdish **ethnic minority**, fleeing **persecution** from Saddam Hussein's government that held power in Iraq until 2003. Many Kurds fear that they will be turned away by customs officers at the airports and ports, so they attempt to enter the UK illegally.

Azad escaped from Iraq in 1998 after Iraqi soldiers threw a grenade into his house, blowing off his right hand. His journey involved week-long treks over freezing mountains in Iran and through forests in Greece. Twelve times, he was crammed into the back of badly-ventilated lorries, barely able to breathe. A Turkish border guard stripped, beat and robbed him.

He crossed the sea from Turkey to Greece on an inflatable raft.

In the final stage of his journey, Azad clung to the underneath of a lorry as it boarded the ferry from France to England. He stayed there throughout the journey. About a mile out of Dover, he dropped to the road and was almost run over by another lorry. He went to the nearest police station and asked for asylum.

Azad has since been granted the status of a 'protected person' and given indefinite leave to remain in the UK. 'No one likes to leave their own country,' he says, 'But if I had remained in Iraq I would have been killed. I hope I can go back one day, but while I'm here in the UK I want to be a useful person, a good member of the community.'

Tibetan refugee children, fleeing persecution in their homeland, take a break on their long trek across the Himalaya Mountains.

Human trafficking

Most refugees cannot afford to pay for their travel to countries as far away as Europe, the USA and Australia. Even if they can scrape together the money for an airline ticket, many airlines refuse to let passengers travel without a visa – an official document allowing them to enter their destination country.

Faced with these problems, many refugees make use of a network of businessmen who give them forged documents, bribe border guards, hide them from the police and smuggle them from one country to another. This business is known as **human trafficking**, and the British Prime Minister Tony Blair describes it as 'the world's fastest-growing criminal business'. Every year, human traffickers help around half a million **immigrants** to enter Europe illegally and 150,000 Mexicans to cross into the USA.

Human trafficking can be very expensive for the refugees. Each stage of the terrible journey undertaken by the Kurdish refugee, Azad, described on page 17 was controlled by a trafficker, and it cost Azad almost £6000. Azad was fortunate that his father, a wealthy merchant, was able to pay the traffickers. Refugees are generally extremely poor. Knowing this, human traffickers do not tend to demand payment up front. Instead, refugees pay in instalments once they are established in a **host country**.

Illegal immigrants

Illegal immigrants must remain hidden from the authorities in their host country, or they will be **deported** (sent back home). They need to earn money, but know that if they attempt to get a job, they will be found by the authorities. There are very few ways to earn money as an illegal immigrant. Crime is one of the handful of options.

Many human traffickers are closely involved with international criminal networks. In 2002, British police uncovered an Albanian crime ring based in Italy. Refugees as young as twelve, from countries such as Romania, were being smuggled first to Italy and then to the UK. They had been given to the traffickers by families, who were hoping that their children would find a better life in the UK. Once the children had been smuggled into the UK, people working for the traffickers stole their papers and their money and forced them to work as criminals – for example, as prostitutes

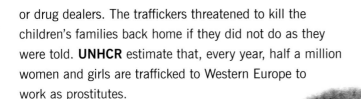

or drug dealers. The traffickers threatened to kill the children's families back home if they did not do as they were told. **UNHCR** estimate that, every year, half a million women and girls are trafficked to Western Europe to work as prostitutes.

A betrayal of trust

Human traffickers force refugees to undertake journeys that are extremely dangerous, and in some cases fatal. In May 2001, fourteen young Mexicans were found dead in the Arizona desert. They had been abandoned by their trafficker 50 kilometres (30 miles) away from any road, with temperatures reaching 54 °C, and no water. There are even cases of traffickers throwing women and children overboard to avoid detection by police boats.

Human traffickers have charged this Kurdish **asylum-seeker** a small fortune to carry him into the European Union by one of the commonest routes – across the sea from Albania into southern Italy. The Italian authorities have found it very hard to stop the flow of refugees on to their shores.

Refugee camps

A major emergency can create a refugee population of hundreds of thousands overnight. The most immediate way in which organizations like **UNHCR** and the International Red Cross can help these refugees is by setting up refugee camps. Many refugee camps are as large as cities. Unlike cities, however, most refugee camps have no sewage system, no regular water supply, no jobs, no shops and no schools.

Refugee camps are designed to be temporary, but they often remain in place for decades. In some parts of the world, children have grown up and had children of their own without ever leaving their camp.

A safe refuge?

Critics of refugee camps argue that they force refugees to be entirely dependent on handouts. One journalist who visited the Nyadeou camp in southern Guinea (Africa) in 2001, described how normally peaceful people were reduced to violent **scavenging** when the food truck arrived.

Refugee camps can easily become filthy, overcrowded and overrun with disease or crime. In many camps, murderers, **guerrillas** and drug smugglers hide themselves among the majority of innocent refugees.

There are numerous examples of armed groups taking control of refugee camps or using them as bases. During conflicts in Central America in the 1980s, guerrillas operated out of refugee camps in Honduras. In the late 1990s, refugee camps in West Timor (Indonesia) provided a place for rebel soldiers to hide.

This well-run refugee camp in central Africa provides vital aid to refugees from Rwanda.

Despite the best efforts of the people that run them, many refugee camps, such as this one in Kosovo, Serbia, become overcrowded, chaotic and dirty.

A possible alternative

One alternative for refugees is to settle in a town or a village and become **integrated** into the local population. This is known as '**self-settlement**'. Several aid agencies argue that self-settlement is in many cases a better option than refugee camps. They say that self-settled refugees can start to rebuild their lives straight away, and are freer and safer than refugees in camps. Oxfam, the Red Cross and many other international aid agencies support programmes in which refugees are helped to self-settle. However, in many areas, the sheer numbers of refugees make self-settlement impossible.

The best solution

Representatives of UNHCR argue that refugee camps are the best way of saving the greatest possible numbers of lives. They point out that it is much easier to help people if they are all gathered in one place. This is certainly true of emergency relief, for instance the distribution of food, water, shelter and medical supplies. It is also true that long-term aid programmes, such as **family tracing**, orphan support and, perhaps most importantly, education, can all be carried out much more easily when refugees are all living together in one place.

Refugees in the media

The last decades of the 20th century saw a huge growth in the use of television and the Internet. This revolution in communications has created a 'global village' in which people all over the world can see what is happening in other parts of the globe. Now, many more people are aware of the problems faced by refugees around the world.

Global campaigns

In 1999, people all over the world could watch on their TV sets what was happening in the Balkans (in south-east Europe). They saw the Serbian army attempt to remove the Albanian people from the province of Kosovo and watched tens of thousands of Albanian Kosovans running for their lives. When the countries of **NATO**, especially the USA and the UK, prepared to defend the Kosovan Albanians by bombing the Serbian army, many people became worried about the safety of the Kosovan refugees. Action groups put pressure on the NATO governments to ensure the safety of the refugees before they dropped any bombs. As a result of this pressure, the USA, the UK, Germany, Italy and Turkey all helped to build refugee camps and worked to return refugees to their homes when the bombing was over.

Today, journalists and film crews highlight the problems of refugees around the world. This TV crew is filming a refugee camp in the Sudan.

The power of the press

In September 2001, people around the world watched a refugee drama unfold. More than 460 refugees fleeing from **civil war** in Afghanistan were stranded on a ship off Christmas Island, an island in the Indian Ocean owned by Australia. Australia's Prime Minister, John Howard, took a tough line, refusing to allow the refugees on to Australian soil.

The refugees were eventually taken to Nauru, a tiny island in the Pacific Ocean. Howard's opponents claimed that he was hiding the refugees from the media. They said that he was worried that media coverage of the refugee story was winning worldwide sympathy for the plight of the boat people and putting pressure on him to let them into Australia.

In recent years, the Australian government has pursued a policy of putting refugees in large detention centres in remote desert regions of the country while their claim for **asylum** is being considered. Many refugees, including hundreds of children, remain in these detention centres for years. In spring 2002, refugees in Australian detention centres went on a hunger strike to protest about their living conditions.

Media coverage of their plight, and publicity campaigns by groups like Oxfam and **Amnesty International**, helped to persuade the Australian authorities to open up the camps for inspection. In July 2002, a **UN** representative named Rajendra Bhagwati visited one camp and, in his report, described the conditions as 'inhuman and degrading'.

When the *Tampa* rescued a group of Afghan **asylum-seekers** from a sinking boat off Christmas Island, the Afghans reportedly threatened to jump overboard if the captain did not take them to Australia. But the Australian government stood firm and refused to allow the ship to dock in Australia.

Refugee or economic migrant?

The authorities in the USA, Europe and Australia deal with hundreds of people every week who arrive without any warning and apply for **asylum**. Whether or not an asylum applicant is given asylum depends largely on whether they fit the 1951 definition of a refugee as someone who 'owing to a well-founded fear of being **persecuted** for reasons of race, religion, nationality, membership of a particular social group, or political opinion, is outside the country of his nationality' (see page 4).

Economic migrants

The most important aspect of the 1951 definition is the threat of persecution. If an applicant cannot prove that they face persecution in their home country, the authorities generally consider that they were not forced to leave their country, but left of their own accord, in search of a better life. Such people are usually classed as '**economic migrants**'.

UNHCR backs up this argument. **Economic** reasons alone are not enough to merit refugee status. Governments of the more developed, richer countries distinguish very carefully between genuine refugees, whose asylum claims they are obliged to accept, and economic migrants, whose claims are generally refused.

Today, there are increasing attempts to crack down on economic migrants who attempt to claim asylum. Economic migrants are often labelled in the popular press as 'asylum-cheats' or '**bogus asylum-seekers**'. However, refugee action groups fear that, as a result, all asylum-seekers will be mistrusted and be suspected of being 'bogus'.

Many asylum-seekers are forced to return home. Here, German authorities deport a group of Romanians, whose claims for asylum have been rejected.

Refugees and poverty

In fact, the distinction between economic migrants and refugees is not always easy to draw. All refugees who arrive in the UK, Australia, Western Europe and the USA, have come from a poorer country and so they all risk being defined as economic migrants.

Poverty may very easily become life-threatening, and force someone to make the refugee's choice to run away or die. The governments of poor countries are less able to protect their citizens than the governments of rich countries, especially in the event of a war or a natural disaster. These governments are also less able to provide their citizens with the basic necessities for survival, such as a regular supply of food, education and healthcare. In some cases, governments deliberately deprive their people of these basic necessities, and keep them in poverty as a way of controlling them. So poverty is one of the reasons why refugees escape from their countries.

Legal papers are very important. This man's papers prove that he is a legal citizen of Bhutan, and is therefore entitled to claim asylum on the grounds of persecution in his homeland.

Asylum-seekers

Many people in the more developed countries believe that it is too easy for illegal **immigrants** to enter a country and claim **asylum**. This is a major source of concern in the USA, Europe and Australia. Illegal immigrants are considered a 'burden on the state'. Because they are unable to work legally, they do not pay taxes and, in many cases, they earn a living from crime.

Border controls

The best defence against illegal immigration is strong border controls – turning people away before they have even entered the country. Once an immigrant is within the country, **deporting** them is an extremely difficult and costly business.

However, numbers of illegal immigrants continue to increase. Tough border controls do not seem to be achieving their aim. Instead, many would-be immigrants are turning to dangerous and expensive **human traffickers** to smuggle them across borders.

Representatives of **UNHCR** argue that strictly-policed borders are shutting out genuine refugees as well as illegal immigrants. This is why genuine refugees are also being forced to turn to human traffickers to help them past borders.

People fleeing from their homes often never manage to get past the borders of their own country. This Afghan girl and her father have been refused permission to cross the border into the relative safety of Pakistan.

Claiming asylum

Many refugees are determined to get to a richer country however hard their journey is. This is partly because, once they have reached a richer country, they have a reasonably good chance of being able to stay there, at least for a while. People claiming asylum are allowed to stay in a country while their claim is considered. Sometimes the government supplies them with an apartment or house and provides welfare payments to cover the rent and basic necessities. However, it is becoming more usual, especially in the UK and Australia, to place large numbers of refugees in detention centres. Even if their claim is rejected, there may be opportunities for them to continue to stay on in their new country, living and working illegally.

In the more developed countries, there is widespread concern that large numbers of **asylum-seekers** are abusing the system. Popular newspapers in countries like the UK, Australia and the USA claim that asylum-seekers are scrounging off their country's generous **benefits** systems.

Yet life as an asylum-seeker is not as attractive as the popular press pictures it to be. In Australia, the USA and many European countries, asylum-seekers are often kept in detention centres indefinitely while their claims are considered. If they are released from the centres, they are placed on 'parole', which means that they must report to the authorities on a regular basis. They are not allowed to work, yet the amount of money paid in benefits does not pay for even life's basic necessities. Many refugee action groups argue that, in some countries, asylum-seekers are treated as though they are criminals, and that in many cases the basic human rights of asylum-seekers are ignored.

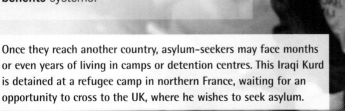

Once they reach another country, asylum-seekers may face months or even years of living in camps or detention centres. This Iraqi Kurd is detained at a refugee camp in northern France, waiting for an opportunity to cross to the UK, where he wishes to seek asylum.

A problem of numbers

A common worry among people in a **host country** is that the refugees will take their jobs and eat their food. In richer countries, negative feelings towards refugees, and any sort of **immigrants**, are based on the idea that each country has a limited number of jobs, houses and land, and that the more people a country takes in, the less there will be to go round. During the Dutch election of 2002, the politician Pim Fortuyn **campaigned** for 'zero immigration' into Holland. Fortuyn was **assassinated** before the election, but his party won huge support for its claim that Holland was 'already a full country'.

Too many refugees?

Yet there is evidence that many people overestimate how many refugees there are. An opinion poll in the UK commissioned to mark the start of Refugee Week in June 2002 found that people believe that the UK takes in nearly 25% of the world's **asylum-seekers**. The true figure is less than 2%.

The sheer numbers of refugees can be overwhelming. Here, a single piece of bread is thrown to thousands of Kosovan refugees, fleeing from Serbian persecution in their homeland.

The truth about refugee movements is that the vast majority flee to countries bordering their home country. The Middle East hosts more than 6 million refugees, and there are over 3.3 million refugees in Africa. The UK received fewer than 80,000 **asylum** claims in 2002, and refused asylum to over 60% of applicants. In 2002, the USA admitted just over 27,000 refugees, an all-time low.

Too few refugees?

Some commentators point out that what the richer countries need is *more* immigrants. The population in these countries is ageing rapidly, and at the same time, birth rates are falling. This means that there are too many pensioners claiming money from the state, and too few people in work earning money and paying taxes. What is needed are people of working age – precisely the category that makes up the majority of asylum-seekers.

Refugees and politics

Representatives of **UNHCR** argue that any refugee's case should be treated purely on the basis of their well-being and basic human rights. However, in practice, the refugee issue is entangled in a number of political concerns.

The Cold War

Between 1945 and 1990, there was open hostility between the USA and its allies, who followed the **capitalist** system of government, and the Soviet Union and its allies, who followed the **communist** system. This situation of hostile stand-off brought the world on several occasions to the brink of war and was known as the Cold War. The Cold War had a great influence on refugee policy, especially in the USA. By welcoming refugees from enemy countries, the US government hoped to cause large numbers of people to leave those countries. The US authorities especially hoped to attract refugees who had worked for the government of an enemy country, believing that these refugees would reveal government secrets and work with the USA to make the enemy government less stable.

Between 1975 and 1999, the USA offered permanent **resettlement** to over 2 million refugees – more than the rest of the world put together. Of these refugees, 1.3 million were from the USA's communist enemies in Asia, especially in Vietnam. The vast majority of the rest were from Cuba and Russia – also communist countries. From the late 1950s to the late 1970s, US law defined a refugee as someone fleeing an enemy country.

Refugees: a vote-losing issue?

Recently, refugee policy throughout the world has become dictated by a different sort of politics – domestic politics. Anti-**immigrant** feeling in Europe and the USA began in the 1970s, when **economic** problems in all these countries meant that jobs, money and houses were scarce. It has never really gone away.

As a result, politicians like the late Pim Fortuyn (see page 28) blame immigrants for a host of social problems – and win a great number of votes. Unfortunately, refugees and immigrants are indistinguishable in many people's eyes. Shutting out refugees is becoming a vote-winning issue, too. After his refusal to let the Afghan boat-people into Australia (see page 23), John Howard's popularity ratings shot up.

He was seen by many Australians as a tough leader who was sticking up for the rights of his people. Later that year, he won the Australian election.

9/11 and immigration

The **terrorist** attacks on New York and Washington in 2001 made anti-immigrant feeling, especially in the USA, much stronger. Many of the terrorists involved had been able to spend considerable time living and working in the USA, planning the attacks, without being picked up by the authorities.

President George W. Bush responded by tightening US immigration controls. But borders that shut out immigrants also shut out refugees. In 2002, the USA accepted just 27,000 refugees. This was tens of thousands fewer than in previous years, and way below the annual target of 70,000 refugees set by the US government.

The failure of the USA, Europe and Australia to separate refugee policy from politics and from their immigration policy represents one of the greatest threats to refugees worldwide.

During the Cold War, the US government welcomed many refugees from communist Vietnam and encouraged them to start a new life in the USA.

❝We must find ways of disentangling refugees from this spreading net of migration controls.❞

Ruud Lubbers, **UN** High Commissioner for Refugees, speaking in 2001

Case study: Elian Gonzalez

It is one of the most famous photographs ever taken: a young refugee cowers in a cupboard, as a US federal agent reaches out for him with one hand and points a machine gun with the other.

Five months before the photograph was taken, on 27 November 1999, fishermen found six-year-old Elian clinging to an inner tube off the coast of Florida. He had been on a boat with twelve other refugees trying to escape from Cuba to the USA. Ten of them, including his mother, had drowned. Over the next six months, young Elian became a legend in his own time.

Different arguments

The US authorities kept Elian Gonzalez in the USA while they considered his case. There were strong arguments for returning Elian to Cuba, and for keeping him in the USA. On the one hand, Elian's mother was dead and his father and the other members of his close family were in Cuba. On the other hand, Elian's mother's dying wish had been to take Elian away from Cuba to the USA.

Cuba is a **communist** country and the USA and Cuba are political enemies, yet only 240 kilometres (150 miles) separate the two countries. Since Fidel Castro came to power in 1959, millions of Cuban refugees have made the dangerous journey across the sea to Florida, in the south-east of the USA, and **exiled** Cubans now make up one third of the residents in Florida's largest city, Miami. The Cuban community in Florida is strongly anti-Castro. They

were determined to stop the American government returning Elian Gonzalez to Cuba. But Cubans in Cuba were equally determined to bring Elian home.

Elian in the media

Media treatment of the case soon reached hysterical proportions. The rights and wrongs of Elian's case became overwhelmed by politics. Anti-Cuban Americans claimed that if Elian was sent home the Cuban government would make his life miserable. Cubans on the island, on the other hand, claimed that Elian had been brainwashed in the USA, and was being turned into a 'toy-obsessed **capitalist**'.

In the end, Elian's father came to the USA and was allowed to take Elian back to Cuba. Whether or not that was the right thing – and what exactly Elian himself wanted – was hard to make out. What is certain is that none of the 4000 unaccompanied children who arrive in the USA every year get as much attention as Elian Gonzalez.

Cuban refugee Elian Gonzalez is discovered hiding in the Miami home of his US relatives. Elian's relatives were determined to keep him in the USA, but his case soon became much more than just a family drama.

Refugees and poverty

Refugee action groups argue that the root cause of the refugee problem is poverty. This is difficult to dispute. The vast majority of refugees run away from poor countries – usually desperately poor countries. Therefore, if wealth were shared out more equally, there would be fewer refugees.

Solving the problem?

There is a worldwide project to share out the world's wealth more equally. It is known as global development. In this process, rich countries try to bring poor countries up to their level. The **campaign** for global development began with the creation of the United Nations after World War II. The **UN**'s mission was underpinned by two basic needs: the need to raise the living standards of the world's deprived people, and the need to make sure that all humans had equal rights.

Yet despite the efforts of the UN, it seems that the global development project is failing. The gap between the rich nations and the poor nations – the 'haves' and the 'have-nots' – is widening dramatically. The UN is also finding it harder to persuade rich countries to help reduce global poverty. At the 1992 Earth Summit in Rio, the rich nations agreed

that a mere 0.7% of their entire annual income should be devoted to Overseas Development Aid (ODA) and in the year 2000, only four nations reached this target. If poorer countries are becoming poorer, it is no wonder that refugee numbers are increasing.

The opposite effect

Some people argue that efforts to make poorer countries richer in fact increase refugee numbers. As countries become more developed, there is a greater movement of goods across their borders. This movement of goods and money across borders makes it easier for

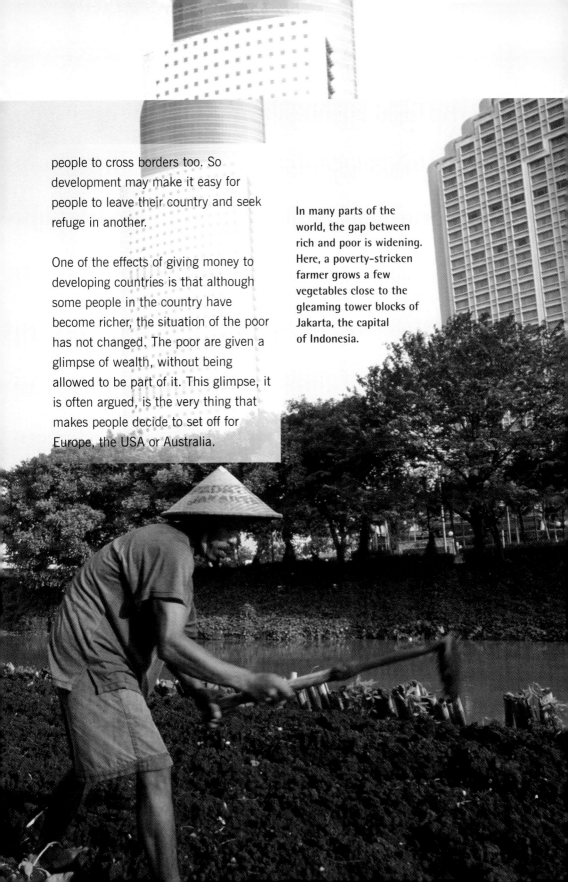

people to cross borders too. So development may make it easy for people to leave their country and seek refuge in another.

One of the effects of giving money to developing countries is that although some people in the country have become richer, the situation of the poor has not changed. The poor are given a glimpse of wealth, without being allowed to be part of it. This glimpse, it is often argued, is the very thing that makes people decide to set off for Europe, the USA or Australia.

In many parts of the world, the gap between rich and poor is widening. Here, a poverty-stricken farmer grows a few vegetables close to the gleaming tower blocks of Jakarta, the capital of Indonesia.

UNHCR

In 1950, the United Nations established the Office of the United Nations High Commissioner for Refugees (**UNHCR**). It had two tasks: to protect refugees, and to find long-term solutions to the problems that cause people to become refugees.

The 1951 Convention

In 1951, delegates from 26 countries met at a UNHCR conference in Geneva. After three weeks of negotiations they finally agreed on the text for the groundbreaking Refugee **Convention** Relating to the Status of Refugees. The Convention established a definition for refugees (see page 4), and set out refugees' rights (see page 7). At first, the Convention was restricted to Europe, but in 1967 it was expanded to include refugees from anywhere in the world; 144 countries have signed the Convention.

IDPs

UNHCR admits that the 1951 Convention definition of a refugee is limited. For example, the Convention states that a refugee is someone who has crossed a national border. Yet in addition to the world's 12 million refugees, there are a further 20–25 million Internally Displaced Persons (**IDPs**) who have fled their homes but have stayed in their own countries. Their situation is as desperate as that of refugees, but under current international law they do not qualify for the same protection as refugees. Currently UNHCR helps 6.3 million IDPs, and works to persuade the international community to provide more assistance to all IDPs.

UNHCR at work

UNHCR staff work in a variety of locations, ranging from regional headquarters in capital cities to remote camps and border areas. At 'ground level', UNHCR workers help refugees to survive their ordeals from day to day. UNHCR programmes are geared

Refugee children on a UNHCR truck in Sri Lanka, the scene of a bitter civil war.

towards helping refugees return to their homeland if this is possible and safe, but they also help people who cannot return home. UNHCR workers help refugees to **integrate** into a new country if they have chosen to **self-settle** or have been granted **asylum**.

In the long term, UNHCR legal and **campaign** teams work to make sure that their own international refugee laws are upheld, and fight to make those laws further-reaching.

UNHCR statistics

Established: 1950

Headquarters: Geneva, Switzerland

Current High Commissioner: Ruud Lubbers (Netherlands) January 2001–

Executive Council: 61 Member States

Offices: 277 offices in 120 countries worldwide

Staff: 5523 (84% working directly with refugees)

Annual Budget: approx. US$880 million

Funding: Under 2% of budget from the **UN**; the rest from voluntary contributions made by governments, corporations and individuals

Major Contributors in 2001:

1. USA (US$245 million)
2. Japan (US$91million)
3. European Commission (US$66 million)
8. UK (US$36 million)
13. Australia (US$12 million).

Source: UNHCR website

UNRWA

At 3.9 million, Palestinian refugees make up the single largest refugee group in the world. Because such large numbers are concentrated in such a small area, they are treated separately from other refugees and have a **UN** agency devoted entirely to them.

This Palestinian boy lives in a refugee camp on the West Bank. He has just received a daily meal provided by UNRWA.

UNRWA runs a training college in Ramallah to provide young Palestinian women with skills that may help them in the future.

The United Nations Relief and Works Agency for Palestine Refugees in the Near East (UNRWA) was founded in 1949 to provide direct relief for the 914,000 refugees of the Arab-Israeli conflict. It was originally designed as a temporary organization, but the Palestinian refugee problem has remained unresolved, and so UNRWA has adjusted its programmes to cater for the long-term needs of four generations of Palestinian refugees.

What UNRWA does

UNRWA works with 1.2 million refugees in 59 camps in Jordan, Lebanon, Syria, the West Bank and the Gaza Strip. Despite the efforts of UNRWA, many of the camps are overcrowded and unhygienic.

Unlike other UN organizations, which work through government authorities, UNRWA provides services directly to the refugees. Major UNRWA programme areas – which would in a normal situation be provided by a government – are education, healthcare, social services and provision of food, medicine and shelter in emergencies.

How it works

UNRWA headquarters are in the Gaza Strip. The Commissioner-General is appointed by the UN Secretary-General and the Advisory Commission. The Advisory Commission meets annually to review Agency activities. Its membership consists of Belgium, Egypt, France, Japan, Jordan, Lebanon, the Syrian Arab Republic, Turkey, the United Kingdom and the United States. The Palestine Liberation Organization, which represents the Palestinian people but is considered by many to be a **terrorist** organization, attends as an observer.

UNRWA has 22,000 staff. Like **UNHCR**, nearly all (95%) of UNRWA funding comes from voluntary contributions from governments and the European Union. In 2002, the UNRWA budget was £200 million. Major government donors were the USA (£66 million), the European Commission (£32 million) and the UK (£15 million). The government of Australia donated £1.6 million.

39

NGOs

Hundreds of organizations throughout the world devote enormous amounts of effort and money to protecting refugees and working for long-term solutions to the refugee problem. These non-governmental organizations are usually known as NGOs. The vast majority of the work carried out by **UNHCR** involves close collaboration with NGOs in both the developed and the developing world.

Emergency relief

UNHCR is one of many organizations that rush to the rescue when **civil war** breaks out, a volcano erupts or the rains fail to arrive. Among them are other **UN** specialized agencies. Rapid response teams from the World Food Programme (WFP) rush emergency food aid to even the remotest regions. The World Health Organization (WHO) provides emergency medical assistance and sets up mass immunization programmes to protect refugees against disease. **UNICEF** (the United Nations Children's Fund) works within refugee camps to protect vulnerable babies and children and provide vital education and healthcare.

The International Committee of the Red Cross (ICRC), together with its sister agency the Red Crescent, is a very important partner in emergency refugee programmes. The Red Cross has been working to help victims of war since 1863, making it one of the oldest NGOs.

The International Organization for Migration (IOM) is another key partner in refugee emergencies. The IOM

For these Ugandan boys, who have been kidnapped and forced to serve as soldiers or slaves, the road to recovery is long and painful. One of the roles of UNICEF is to help troubled children enjoy their lives once more.

specializes in the transportation of refugees and **IDPs** away from crisis areas, and also helps refugees returning to their own countries to rejoin their societies.

Campaigning for change

All of the groups described above are joined by hundreds of organizations around the world in the **campaign** to protect refugees. **Amnesty International** is the best known of many pressure groups throughout the world. In Australia, for example, Amnesty's National Refugee Team works to persuade the Australian government to protect refugees' rights and to carry out a refugee **asylum** policy in

accordance with the terms of the 1951 UNHCR **Convention**.

Some NGOs launch awareness campaigns in the press, on TV and on the Internet to publicize the desperate situation of refugees. The US Committee for Refugees, for example, through its annual *World Refugee Survey*, conducts a sustained campaign to promote the cause of refugees worldwide and to record abuses of human rights in refugee situations. In the UK, the Refugee Council provides advice and support to **asylum-seekers** and refugees living in the UK. It offers training and employment courses, and works with refugee community organizations throughout the country.

A convoy of Red Cross trucks bring vital food aid to starving people in Ethiopia. Without this aid, thousands would die.

Caring for children

The total number of refugee children, including those forced out of their homes but still in their own countries, may currently be as high as 25 million. It is a sad fact that children, especially babies and infants, often suffer the most in emergency situations. These situations are not only beyond their control, but also beyond their understanding.

In September 2002, Carol Bellamy, Executive Director of **UNICEF**, addressed the **UNHCR** Executive Committee. 'To spend even a day in a refugee camp is too long for a child; yet, we know that children live in these camps for years – and, in some cases, for generations ... we are talking about a state of affairs that involves violations of so many child rights that I lack the time to list them all.'

UNICEF and UNHCR work together very closely on programmes targeted at children in refugee camps. One key focus area is counselling to help children cope with the **trauma** of war. A 1995 study found that 75% of Rwandan children had witnessed relatives being murdered, and 42% had seen children killing other children. (For more information about the **civil war** in

These refugee children live in an abandoned train wagon in Azerbaijan, central Asia.

Rwanda, see page 15). In 2000, a study in Kabul, Afghanistan, found that after years of war, over 40% of children felt that life was not worth living, and 90% had terrifying nightmares.

Case study
Children in war

In Jabalia refugee camp, on the Palestinian-run Gaza strip, Manal, aged fourteen, holds up the picture she has been working on for the past hour. It shows a deep blue sky, birds, flowers and children playing in a field. In the corner of the picture is a man. 'He's telling them to be careful about bombs and gunfire,' says Manal.

Until recently, Manal and thousands of other children in the Jabalia camp have had few outlets to express their fears and hopes for the future. Because of the dramatic increase in conflict in the region since September 2000 there has been little opportunity for fun and play.

The 'Children and Future' project, supported by UNICEF, began on 7 October 2001. Under this project, children take part in discussions, art classes and drama workshops. This gives them an opportunity to work out some of their fears and anxieties about their daily lives and reflect on their thoughts about the future. For many refugee children who are suffering trauma as a result of conflict, this is a crucial first step on the road to recovery. UNICEF also helps teachers, health workers, families and other community members to understand and fulfil the needs of these children.

Life can be very hard for children living in refugee camps. Here, the Jabalia refugee camp in the Gaza Strip spills on to a disused railway line.

Repatriation

Repatriation means 'returning to the homeland'. Most refugees want to return home if it is safe to do so. **Voluntary repatriation** of refugees is the ultimate goal of **UNHCR**, but it is only possible if there is a long-term solution to the problem that has caused the refugees to run in the first place.

Returning to Afghanistan

Civil war has raged in Afghanistan since the early 1970s. During this period, Afghanistan has been a major source of the world's refugees. The cycles of war have often been made worse by terrible **droughts**. In 1990, numbers of Afghan refugees reached a horrifying peak of 6.2 million. In 2002, the figure was 3.9 million.

The vast majority of Afghan refugees now live in neighbouring Pakistan and Iran. However, a great many refugees – currently around a million – are uprooted from their homes, but are still within the borders of Afghanistan.

In 2001, following the **terrorist** attacks on New York and Washington, the USA and its allies bombed Afghanistan. They believed that Osama bin Laden, the man suspected of masterminding the attacks, was hiding there. The refugee situation in Afghanistan – already serious – threatened to become one of the worst disasters in human history, as hundreds of thousands of people left their homes and ran for their lives.

The Talibaan government of Afghanistan soon fell and the new president, Hamid Karzai, immediately laid the ground for the return of refugees. The **UN** repatriation began on 1 March 2002. UNHCR estimated that 800,000 of the 4 million Afghan refugees in Pakistan and Iran would return during the year, but that target had been reached within 15 weeks. By mid-year, 1.2 million refugees and 400,000 **IDPs** had returned home. A parallel operation by **UNICEF** saw 1.5 million children go back to school – many of them for the first time in 6 years.

But although this situation is encouraging in many ways, UNHCR has warned there may be serious problems. Drought and internal conflicts are still major threats in Afghanistan, and there are an estimated 7 million unexploded landmines throughout the country. Afghans returning home late in the year face a struggle to survive in the freezing winter.

Avoiding refoulement

Repatriation of **asylum-seekers** is a very good solution for **host countries**, because it reduces their burden. Pakistan and Iran worked hard to help Afghans return home.

Around 150,000 Afghans applied for **asylum** in 90 countries around the world between 1999 and 2002. Many countries urged Afghans to take voluntary repatriation. However, there is a danger that, in their haste to repatriate refugees, host countries will send them back to violence and **persecution**. Returning someone to their home country against their will is known as *refoulement*, and it is forbidden by the 1951 UNHCR **Convention**.

After nearly three years living in a refugee camp on the border with Zaire (the Democratic Republic of the Congo), these refugees are finally returning home to Rwanda.

Individual campaigners

The exile: the Dalai Lama

The mountainous country of Tibet has long struggled to be independent from its powerful neighbour, China. In 1950, 80,000 Chinese troops invaded Tibet. The Chinese government announced that Tibet was part of China, and its army killed or imprisoned any Tibetans who disagreed. Tens of thousands of Tibetans ran for their lives.

When the Chinese took over Tibet, the Dalai Lama, Tibet's spiritual and political leader, was only fifteen years old. He stayed in Tibet and tried to find a way of living peacefully with the Chinese. However, in 1959, he escaped across the Himalayas and set up a government in **exile** in Dharamsala, northern India. The Dalai Lama is still in exile, and by 2002 the community of Tibetan refugees had grown to 130,000.

The Dalai Lama's message of peace and non-violence has won him admiration all over the world. In 1989 he won the Nobel Peace Prize, which he accepted 'on behalf of the oppressed everywhere'.

In October 2002, the Dalai Lama made a donation of US$50,000 to **UNHCR** to help Afghan refugees.

Pictured in 2000, Tibetan spiritual leader the Dalai Lama raises his hands in a traditional gesture of greeting.

> **"**During my first visit to the field, I expected to meet people who were very different from me. What I learned on my visit is that although we don't speak the same language or share the same culture, refugees are just like you and me. They want the same things we all do.**"**
>
> Angelina Jolie, in a speech in Washington DC on World Refugee Day, 20 June 2002

Angelina Jolie meets girls from Sierra Leone on a visit to a refugee camp. The girls had been forced to flee their homes as a result of local wars.

The celebrity: Angelina Jolie

American actress Angelina Jolie, who won an Oscar in 2000 for her role in *Girl, Interrupted*, is a deeply committed **campaigner** on behalf of refugees. In February and March 2001, Jolie took a trip to visit refugees under the care of **UNHCR** in Sierra Leone and Tanzania, West Africa. She has since visited refugees fleeing from conflicts all over the world. She visited Afghans living in camps in Pakistan two weeks before the American bombing of Afghanistan.

Angelina Jolie has made her experiences public, publishing a diary which provides honest, heartfelt insights into how refugees live and how the refugee system operates. Her fame attracts a lot of publicity to the cause, and she shows a courage and generosity that would be beyond many people. In August 2001, she was made a **UN** Goodwill **Ambassador**, joining a group of leading personalities from the worlds of art, music, film, sport, literature and public affairs who help to publicize key United Nations issues and activities.

What can I do?

The world can seem a very bleak place. The statistics for refugees are difficult to comprehend – tens of thousands dead, millions on the run ... and yet, wherever there is despair, there may also be hope. Thousands of people throughout the world show heroism and passion in their selfless work for refugees. If you are moved by what you have read in this book you may be inspired to become involved in helping refugees yourself.

Working with refugees can be a very positive experience. This volunteer is helping children to readjust to normal life again, after a long period of living as refugees.

> **❝**Members and officials of Europe ... if you see that we have sacrificed and risked our lives, it is because there is too much suffering in Africa and we need you to struggle against poverty and put an end to war in Africa.**❞**
>
> Extract from a letter discovered on the bodies of two fourteen-year-old boys from Guinea, West Africa, who were found dead in the landing gear of a plane at Brussels Airport in 1999

Helping refugees

A number of charities – such as Oxfam, **Amnesty International** and Christian Aid – undertake either regular work or one-off appeals for refugees fleeing from wars, **persecution** or natural disasters in the developing world. Their work is supported by hundreds of lesser-known charities. There are also many organizations working to ensure fair treatment for refugees and **asylum-seekers** in **host countries**, offering counselling, legal advice and a support network.

If you are of working age, perhaps your skills could be of value. Many charities welcome volunteers. If you are not of working age, maybe you have something you can donate, which you don't need any more but which will make a great difference to someone else's life. There are some useful addresses on pages 52–53.

Remember: a refugee is not just a stranger thousands of miles away. A refugee may be your classmate, your neighbour or even your teacher. If we listen to what people have to say before we judge them, then the world may not seem so bleak after all.

I am a refugee

There are several organizations that serve the interests of refugees and asylum-seekers in industrialized countries. If you are a refugee or asylum-seeker, if you fear that your case is not being given a fair hearing, or your rights are not being respected, if you are experiencing violence or prejudice, or if you are lonely and unhappy, contact them: they exist to help you. Addresses are on pages 52–53.

Facts and figures

Refugee numbers

This table shows which countries produced the most refugees in 2002.

Country of Origin	Total	Main Countries of Asylum
Afghanistan	3,810,000	Pakistan, Iran
Burundi	554,000	Tanzania
Iraq	530,000	Iran
Sudan	490,000	Uganda, Ethiopia, Democratic Republic of the Congo
Angola	471,000	Zambia, Democratic Republic of the Congo, Namibia
Somalia	440,000	Kenya, Yemen, Ethiopia, USA, UK
Bosnia-Herzegovina	426,000	Yugoslavia, USA, Sweden, Denmark, Netherlands
Democratic Rep. Congo	392,000	Tanzania, Democratic Republic of the Congo, Zambia, Rwanda, Burundi
Vietnam	353,000	China, USA
Eritrea	333,000	Sudan

Host countries

These are the countries that are currently hosting the most refugees:

1. Pakistan — 2,000,000
2. Iran — 1,900,000
3. Germany — 906,000
4. Tanzania — 681,000
5. USA — 507,000
6. Yugoslavia — 484,000
7. Guinea — 433,000
8. Sudan — 401,000
9. Democratic Republic of the Congo — 332,000
10. China — 294,000

Refugee percentages

These countries have the highest percentage of refugees in their population:

1. Armenia — 8.4%
2. Guinea — 6.8%
3. Yugoslavia — 4.7%
4. Djibouti — 3.7%
5. Liberia — 3.3%
6. Azerbaijan — 2.9%
7. Iran — 2.7%
8. Zambia — 2.3%
9. Tanzania — 1.9%
10. Sweden — 1.8%

Increasing numbers

In the second half of the 20th century, numbers
of refugees worldwide increased tenfold:

1951	2,100,000
1961	1,500,000
1971	2,800,000
1981	10,200,000
1991	17,000,000
2001	21,100,000

Asylum applications

This table shows which industrialized countries received the most asylum
applications in 2001.

Country of Asylum	Number of Claims	Main Countries of Origin
UK	88,300	Afghanistan, Iraq, Somalia, Sri Lanka
Germany	88,290	Iraq, Turkey, Yugoslavia, Afghanistan, Russian Federation
USA	86,180	Mexico, China, Colombia, Haiti, Armenia
France	47,290	Turkey, Democratic Republic of the Congo, China, Mali, Algeria
Canada	44,040	Hungary, Pakistan, Sri Lanka, Zimbabwe, China
Netherlands	32,580	Angola, Afghanistan, Sierra Leone, Iran
Austria	30,140	Afghanistan, Iraq, Turkey, India
Belgium	24,550	Russian Federation, Yugoslavia, Algeria, Democratic Republic of the Congo, Iran
Sweden	23,520	Iraq, Yugoslavia, Bosnia-Herzegovina
Switzerland	20,630	Yugoslavia, Turkey, Bosnia-Herzegovina, Iraq

Further information

International organizations

UNHCR (The Office of the United Nations High Commission for Refugees)
www.unhcr.ch

UNRWA (United Nations Relief and Works Agency for Palestine Refugees in the Near East)
www.un.org/unrwa

UNICEF (United Nations Children's Fund)
www.unicef.org

International Organization for Migration (IOM)
www.iom.int

European Council on Refugees and Exiles
www.ecre.org

Global IDP Project (Project to help Internally Displaced Persons)
www.idpproject.org/

International Committee of the Red Cross
www.icrc.org

International Federation of Red Cross and Red Crescent Societies
www.ifrc.org

Human Rights Watch
www.hrw.org/refugees

Contacts in the UK and Ireland

British Home Office Immigration and Nationality Directorate
Lunar House
40, Wellesley Road
Croydon CR9 2BY
Tel: 0870 606 7766
www.ind.homeoffice.gov.uk

The Refugee Council UK
Head Office
3 Bondway
London SW8 1SJ
Tel: 020 7820 3000
www.refugeecouncil.org.uk

Irish Refugee Council
40 Lower Dominick Street
Dublin 1
Eire
Tel: 01 8730042
www.irishrefugeecouncil.ie

New Vision
an online publication by refugees for refugees
www.newvision.org.uk

Refugee Legal Centre
Sussex House
39-45 Bermondsey Street
London, SE1 3XF
Tel : 020 7827 9090
www.rlcuk.demon.co.uk

OXFAM
Oxfam House
274 Banbury Road
Oxford OX2 7DZ
Tel: 01865 312610
www.oxfam.org.uk

Save the Children UK
17 Grove Lane
London SE5 8RD
Tel: 020 7703 5400
www.scfuk.org.uk

Contacts in the USA

Bureau of Citizenship and Immigration Services
425 I ('Eye') Street, NW
Washington, DC 20536
Tel: 1-800-375-5283
www.immigration.gov

Department of Health and Human Services, Office of Refugee Resettlement (ORR)
Administration for Children and Families
370 L'Enfant Promenade, SW
6th Floor
Washington, DC 20447
Tel: 202-401-9246
www.acf.hhs.gov

Social Security Online
(Immigration Office of Public Inquiries)
Windsor Park Building
6401 Security Blvd.
Baltimore, MD 21235
Tel: 1-800-772-1213
www.ssa.gov

US Commission for Refugees
1717 Massachusetts Ave. NW
Suite 200
Washington, DC 20036
Tel: 202-347-3507
www.refugees.org

American Refugee Committee (ARC)
2344 Nicollet Ave. South
Suite 350
Minneapolis, MN 55404
Tel: 612-872-7060
www.archq.org

Contacts in Canada

Citizenship and Immigration Canada
P.O. Box 7000
Sydney, Nova Scotia B1P 6V6
Tel: 1-888-242-2100
cicnet.ci.gc.ca

Canadian Council for Refugees
6839 Drolet #302
Montréal, Québec, H2S 2T1
Canada
Tel: 514-277-7223
www.web.net/~ccr

Contacts in Australia

Minister for Immigration and Multiracial Affairs
Parliament House
Canberra, ACT 2600
Tel: 02-6277-7860
www.minister.immi.gov.au/index.htm

Refugee Action Committee
LPO Box A287
ANU
Canberra, ACT 2601
Tel: 04-1575-2012
www.refugeeaction.org

Refugee Council of Australia
PO Box 946
Glebe 2037
NSW
Tel: 02-9660-5300
www.refugeecouncil.org.au

Contacts in New Zealand

New Zealand Immigration Service
Private Bag
Wellesley Street
Auckland
Tel: 0508-558-855
www.immigration.govt.nz

Glossary

ambassador
someone who works internationally to promote the interests of their country, organization or set of beliefs

Amnesty International
international organization that campaigns for people imprisoned or unfairly treated because of their beliefs

assassinate
to murder an important person, such as a president

asylum
protection given by one country to a refugee from another, allowing them to attempt to build a new life free from fear of violence or persecution

asylum-seeker
refugee or would-be refugee who is asking the government of another country to provide them with a safe place to live

benefits
payments made by a government to people who are unable to work

bogus
false, or pretend

campaign
to take action over a period of time in order to achieve something

capitalism
way of organizing a country so that all the land, factories etc. belong to private individuals, rather than to the state

citizenship
official membership of a particular country. Citizens have certain duties, rights, and privileges.

civil war
war fought by rival groups within one country

communism
way of organizing a country so that everything belongs to the state and the profits are shared out among everyone

consulate
office representing a nation or state within a foreign country

convention
international agreement

deport
to expel someone from a country

discriminate
to treat people differently according to their gender, race, religious or political beliefs

displaced
forced to leave home

drought
long period of very dry weather during which crops fail

economic
referring to money in society

economic migrant
someone who has chosen to move from one country to another in order to improve their financial circumstances

embassy
office representing a nation or state within a foreign country

ethnic group
group of people who share the same ancestors and traditions

ethnic minority
group within a country whose racial or cultural background is different from that of the majority in that country

exile
to force someone to leave their home country

exodus
departure of a large number of people

family tracing
programme run in refugee camps by aid agencies to help children and families who have become separated to be reunited

guerrilla
soldier in an unofficial army that typically operates in small bands and launches surprise attacks

host country
country in which a refugee finds temporary or permanent refuge

human trafficking
illegal transporting of people from one country to another, in return for payment

IDP
initials standing for Internally Displaced Person: a person who has been forced to flee their home but has not crossed a border into another country

immigrant
someone who has left one country and settled permanently in another

integrate
to become a part of something

legal status
way a person is viewed by the law-enforcers of a country and the rights they have according to those laws

NATO
initials standing for North Atlantic Treaty Organization: an international body created in 1949 to safeguard the security of its members, who include the USA, Canada and seventeen European countries

Nazis
short name for the German Nationalist Socialist Workers' Party, led by Adolf Hitler, who ruled Germany from 1933 to 1945

persecute
to treat a person with violence or prejudice for racial, religious or political reasons. In many cases, persecution ends in the death of the person or people persecuted.

Prussia
powerful German state that existed until 1947

psychoanalyst
someone who studies people's minds and the ways that they behave

resettlement
process by which refugees or immigrants are moved to a new society or country and are helped to integrate

scavenge
to search among rubbish for food or something useful

self-settlement
process by which refugees move to a new society or country and integrate of their own accord

Secretary of State (US)
one of the most senior government positions, with responsibility for foreign policy

terrorist
someone who uses violence for political reasons

trauma
deep shock, usually emotional

UN
initials standing for United Nations: an international body set up in 1945 to promote international peace and cooperation

UNHCR
initials standing for the Office of the High Commissioner for Refugees: an international body set up by the UN in 1950 to deal with refugees

UNICEF
initials standing for the United Nations Children's Fund: an international body set up by the UN to help children in need

voluntary repatriation
process by which refugees are helped to return to their own country, because this is what they want

Index

Titles in the *Just the Facts* series include:

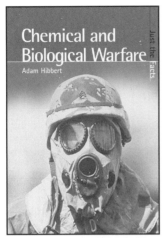

Chemical and Biological Warfare
Adam Hibbert

Hardback   0 431 16160 7

Child Labour
Kaye Stearman

Hardback   0 431 16161 5

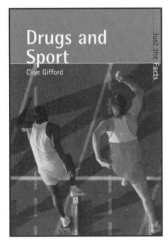

Drugs and Sport
Clive Gifford

Hardback   0 431 16162 3

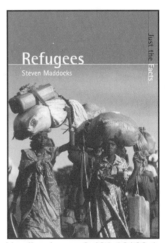

Refugees
Steven Maddocks

Hardback   0 431 16163 1

Sustainable Development
Clive Gifford

Hardback   0 431 16164 X

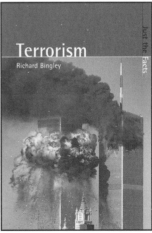

Terrorism
Richard Bingley

Hardback   0 431 16165 8

Find out about the other titles in this series on our website www.heinemann.co.uk/library